DIGGING DEEPER

Complied by: Coletta Bethea

Contributing Authors

Coletta Bethea

D'Jare Campbell

Quantissa Smith

Beverly Davis

Tatecca Allen

Denysha Lavelle

CONTENTS

ACKNOWLEDGEMENTS & DEDICATION

To the amazing women who saw it not robbery to take the time to share their stories of growth from battles and trials that so many have faced but were afraid to share, I thank you.

This book is dedicated to anyone who needs just that little bit of encouragement to push through difficult situations and trying times.

To my precious grandbabies for giving me a reason to keep fighting.

INTRODUCTION

There comes a time in life when you have to realize what is for you and what isn't. So why do we try to force people and/or things in our lives that truly does not fit? Why are we so stuck on surface level things? Why is it so hard for us to go beyond the surface?

It's like buying clothes, you wouldn't purposely buy clothes that don't fit, right? If you are in store looking for an outfit and you see one in a size smaller than what you wear, you would *Dig* through or search for your correct size, right? So why is it so hard for us to Dig Deeper in finding ourselves, our purpose, or our calling? See, what I'm saying is wearing stuff that doesn't fit ultimately makes you look foolish.

That reminds me, why do we keep things that we no longer need? It served a purpose in a specified time frame. Now, it's either to small, to big, has holes or faded? So, tell me again why it is still hanging in your closet! Do you recall your mother doing spring and winter cleaning? She's Digging Deep into her closet to see what she needs to keep and/or discard.

If you are following me, you'll know I'm not necessarily talking about clothes, I'm really referring to things and people in your life.

We have the tendency to hold on to people and things that we should have released eons ago?

Why are you still being loyal to them? What are you benefiting from holding on to it (them)? What substance is it/they bringing to your life, your dreams, your goals? Are they pushing you to become a better version of you?

Are the clothes in your wardrobe that has holes in it a representation of who you are? Would you wear it to a business meeting? Would you wear a shirt that is too small or the extra-large shoes to show up to the office every day? The straight up answer is No! So why in the world do we drown ourselves the baggage that is not beneficial to our growth and wellbeing instead of digging up things that does not belong or cannot help us grow.

As I sat back and reviewed all these unanswered and some rhetorical questions it caused me to DIG DEEPER into who I was, who I am and who I am becoming. As I began to look back over specific time frames in my life, I realized I held on to things and people I should have let go a long time ago! I know I'm not the only one. When you begin to dig deeper you find yourself and who God has called you to be and what He purposes you to do. When you begin to Dig Deeper you realize that old dirt, old baggage and old things will not help you grow but only hinder you from becoming your true authentic self. Scripture says, "Men do not put new wine into old skin bags. If they did, the skins would break and the wine would run out. The bags would be no good. They put new wine into new skin bags and both can be used" *Matthew 9:17 NLV*.

Digging Deeper takes courage. Digging Deeper takes faith. Digging Deeper takes determination. Are you willing to give all of these things to dig deeper to find you?

In the next few chapters, you'll hear from women from all walks of life. They will share their stories of life and how Digging Deeper into their purpose and calling has shifted them to another level.

"He is like a man building a house, who dug deep and laid the foundation on the rock. And when a flood arose, the stream broke against that house and could not shake it, because it had been well built."

Luke 6:48 ESV

oletta Bethea, native of SC and faith-based author, speaker, coach and educator and a mom of two. She's a graduate of Limestone University. She currently holds an AA degree in Liberal Studies, BA degree in Psychology and currently pursing he MA in Special Education with a concentration in Autism. She thrives on education and women empowerment. Coletta prides herself on educating children with autism and helping women overcome internal emotional battles, giving birth to books, and offering women empowerment workshops and speaking engagements. Coletta is dedicated to helping women find their passion and understanding their purpose through biblical and life experiences. She thrives on knowing that every woman who crosses her path has a better understanding of who they were created and destine to be.

I SHALL LIVE AND NOT DIE

Warm water filled my eyes, as I sat and reminisced on life and all of the things I've been through, the good the bad, the ugly. Growing up I was raised in church. I knew the Lord; I had a relationship with him. I gave my life to Christ at a young age. (Who would have ever thought I would be here?) Now that doesn't say I did everything right. But I knew my foundation had been set early on. As I aged, I strayed from the path that I was taught. Having two children by the age of 20, one that wasn't consensual, not being married, entangled in horrible relationships, daddy issues, dead end jobs, church hurt and family issues. I was on a downward spiraling whirlwind.

I couldn't see any farther for my life than the stop sign at the end of road. The hope I had of myself was tarnished, my purpose was blurred. The vision for my life seemed impossible. How could I do anything at this point. Depression sank in. How can this be happening to me?

Years of dealing with this illness, crying late nights, waking up smiling and going to work each day like everything was ok, was putting more of a toll on me. I was a functioning depressive, and no one even knew it, not even my closest friends. The smile I wore was fake, it was phony, it was a cover up for every time some asked me if I was ok. Years passed and the pain began to become unbearable. I couldn't take it anymore. I decided it was time. I prepared my legal documents. I prayed for forgiveness in advance. I asked God to cover my children and my family. I was ready. As I laid in my bed pills in hand, rolled in fetal position, I sobbed. This had to happen it was the only way to get through all of life's disappointments. I drifted into a deep sleep.

Upon awaking from the much-needed rest, I heard the small voice "You will live and not die." It takes strength, courage and most importantly trust in God to become who He has created you to be. It's not easy. You will have trials and tribulations, but you have to be able to withstand the fire, the pruning and the pressing. In the end there is victory if you just believe.

Depression is an illness that not many people talk about and go through alone because they are afraid of being judged. I was that person. I was taught to be strong, pray and everything would be ok. Sometimes life can throw some fast hard balls, some of which you cannot catch and throw back. When those balls hit you if feels as if your entire life has ended. Your body is bruised, your mind is tired, and your heart is broken. At that moment I thought my life was over, I felt as if all hope was lost. I asked myself, "How did I get here?" But no matter how hard life may seem dig deep into your soul, remember who you are and whose you are. Never allow the enemy to cloud your mind with thoughts of defeat. Push through and change your mindset and your way of thinking about yourself. One thing I learned along this journey is it is ok to seek professional help. Sometimes we have to have medication to help us overcome sickness in our bodies and in our minds. Surround yourself with positive people. Find a support group where you can share and hear other testimonies. You don't have to go through life and especially hard situations alone. Use the experience as a steppingstone to get to your next level. Never allow fear to stop you from receiving the help that you need to pull you back to the place where you belong. You were put here for a purpose! If you didn't have purpose on your life the enemy wouldn't fight you so hard to stop you from reaching your destiny! You will live and not die! Is there anything that can help you overcome these hardships (you wonder)? My answer is yes there is.

Scripture

Matthew 11:28-30 GW

"Come to me, all who are tired from carrying heavy loads, and I will give you rest. Place my yoke [a] over your shoulders, and learn from me, because I am gentle and humble. Then you will find rest for yourselves because my yoke is easy, and my burden is light."

Questions to Ponder:

What heavy loads are you caring?

_____

_____

_____

_____

_____

_____

How do you get to the place of bouncing back after so many hard hits?

_____

_____

_____

_____

_____

_____

Do you trust Christ to give you the peace and rest that you desire and need?

_____

_____

_____

_____

_____

_____

Prayer

Heavenly Father, I pray for the person reading this story. I pray that you cover their hearts and minds whenever they feel that that have nothing to live for and remind them that they have you. Remind them that your strength is made perfect in their weakness and that you will carry them through the storms of life. Remind them that they do not have to go through this alone. Give them strength to push through the hard times and the difficult seasons of life. Father put people in their lives that will nurture them, pray for them, and help build them up in hard times. Give them the heart and mind to forgive themselves as the continue to move forward in their purpose and pursuit of life.

Reflection

_____

_____

_____

_____

_____

_____

_____

_____

_____

_____

_____

_____

_____

_____

_____

_____

_____

_____

_____

_____

_____

_____

"It is in Him that we live and move and keep on living. Some of your own men have written, 'We are God's children."
Acts 17:28 NL

D'Jare Campbell is a Columbia, SC native, author and graduate of Benedict College. Her mission is to end toxic relationship cycles in order to build strong family-oriented communities. This mission led her to publish *The 24 Hour Rule: Determining Your Dating Partner's Marriage Potential in 30 Days*. It is the most talked about, faith-based relationship manual since its release in January 2019. This Woman's Worth Strategist encourages women to "Seek ascension, not attention" when dating. Whether you find her speaking and teaching at live events or online, her lasting message will be: "You CANNOT date the world's way and expect Kingdom results."

LORD, HELP ME TO LOVE AGAIN

"**A**LL men are dogs! I don't want anyone else's son offering to open my door. NO! ...I'm not giving another man my phone number... and if another man attempts to look in my direction with that silly grin on his face, I will make him regret it," I screamed. You should have seen me on my full-blown emotional rant with my face drenched in tears. I'd had enough. It seemed as if I kept meeting the same men with different names. At one point, I convinced myself to date men out-of-state. Yet, there I was again, sitting in front of my girlfriends hysterically crying over another man. "HA! What a joke. The men out-of-state are just as trifling as those other clowns I'm used to," I continued to sob in self-pity. My girlfriends intently listened to my pity party while drying my tears. Moments later, my neighbors would be privileged to overhear the 3-hour male-bashing session that followed.

After fussing until my voice crackled and barely any saliva remained in my mouth, I finally did the one thing I should have done from the start- HUSH and talk to God. For the first time ever, I sincerely prayed. It wasn't just any ol' memorized repetitive prayer either. It was a prayer that came from the depths of my heart. It was a humble request for God to show me what I was doing wrong in my relationships. I desperately needed answers. My unborn children desperately needed this toxic cycle to end.

Instead of receiving the easy answers I desired, God revealed one of the root causes of my relationship issues- sexual assault. When I was a little girl, I didn't know what happened- or rather what almost happened- had a name. I only knew what *he* tried to do to me was wrong. No little girl should be forcefully pushed against a wall, touched inappropriately, or told explicit plans. A little girl shouldn't have to fight off someone she once enjoyed playing with in order to protect her innocence. A little girl shouldn't feel as if sharing her secret would result in more harm than good.

That day, someone opened the door just after he said those words I will never forget: "No one can save you now." When that door opened, I ran through it like an Olympic Sprinter. "I was saved," I thought as I panted to catch my breath. As I heard God speak to me the night I prayed, I was led to dig deeper into how I interacted with men. I discovered that though I was physically saved from rape, I was not saved from how I viewed males after that day. How I interacted with boys/men was no longer the same. The world I imagined to be full of sunshine, rainbows and clouds that tasted like my favorite flavor of cotton candy, now became a dangerous place. The boys I used to playfully wrestle were now instant enemies. The handsome princes I read about who wanted to marry the girl they loved were now thought of as just characters in a fantasy book. I believed good men didn't exist. Therefore, I either didn't trust that the good men I met were genuine or I ran them away. I know my life's events will not necessarily speak for everyone who may have had similar experiences. However, I encourage you to also hush and sincerely talk to God about your relationship challenges. Your request just may expose a root cause that must be destroyed.

Scripture

And now abide faith, hope, love, these three; but the greatest of these is love.

Questions to Ponder:

Do you believe good men exist and that he would want to Love you?

_____

_____

_____

_____

_____

Do you accuse your boyfriend of betrayal when he doesn't call you at the exact time, he says he will?

_____

_____

_____

_____

_____

_____

Do you question if your boyfriend really loves you when he actually treats you with respect and spends time with you regularly?

_____

_____

_____

_____

_____

_____

Prayer

Lord, forgive me for my sins as I forgive those who have hurt me physically and/or emotionally.

I desire a healthy relationship with the man in whom you are well-pleased. May my desire align with Your desire. Help me to heal the pieces of my heart that I am afraid to revisit. May every root of fear and doubt that Love is real be destroyed.

In Jesus' name I pray, Amen.

Reflection

_____

_____

_____

_____

_____

_____

_____

_____

_____

_____

_____

_____

_____

_____

_____

_____

_____

_____

_____

_____

_____

_____

_____

_____

_____

_____

_____

_____

"There is no fear in love. Perfect love puts fear out of our hearts."
1ˢᵗ John 4:18 NLV

Quantissa Smith was born in Wiesbaden Germany and is the mother of one amazing daughter, Trynity. Ms. Smith was born to be Authentic, and her name is a symbol of her authenticity. She is the visionary behind the vision of Authentic Artistry Phase 2 LLC. Quantissa is a home decor & design Specialist, Educator and Author. As the scripture says, "her gifts are making room for her". Each day she purposes to show the love of Christ by "Getting Up" ... "Getting Cute"... "Being Present" for purpose.

DON'T SHRINK BACK

ele

"And in love he chose us before he laid the foundation of the universe! Because of his great love, he ordained us, so that we would be seen as holy in his eyes with an unstained innocence."
Ephesians 1:4 TPT

Looking past the surface and digging deeper into who you are divine to be. This is digging deeper

Note to Self

"You deserve to be you."~Quantissa

"Before I Shaped you in the womb, I knew all about you. Before you saw the light of day, I had holy plans for you: a prophet to the nations- that's what I had in mind for you" Jeremiah 1:5

Just sit back and think how important you are in the mind of Christ. That he thought of you before the creations of the earth. I know and understand that now as I'm becoming fully single. Single meaning pure, separate, whole and unique. Pure before God. Separate from the way the world or culture say we are supposed to be. Whole meaning to be complete in Christ; understanding that you have been made righteous by believing.

Unique it's okay to be different because there is no one else on earth just like you.

Focusing on uniqueness and knowing just who you've been designed to be. A lot of time when we don't know who we are we shrink back from the person God designed and called us to be. When we shrink back, you'll find yourself copying the trends of culture and not kingdom. When we lose focus and it's no longer on God and who He designed us to be. We try to please others and lose who we are. Our focus has changed from the destiny and purpose God didn't create us to try to please others and become a copy of them. What does shirking back mean? To shrink is defined: is to move back or away, especially because of fear or disgust. To draw back or retreat. What would cause you to draw back or retreat? Your past hurts, fear, wanting to please others and sin.

A lot of times when we start to dig deeper into our purpose, fear of the unknown causes us to shrink. The response of people causes us to shrink back. What will someone say cause us to shrink back? Our past will cause us to shrink. We choose to retreat to what is comfortable to us.

On this journey of becoming the Authentic Me I had to first start seeking the face of God with every decision I made. I can remember the many times I shrink back because I didn't believe in the person God designed me to be. I would worry about what others would or won't say because of my flaws, mistakes, and sins. Or how I would second guess the gifts and talents God had given me. Even though I know His word reminds me that my gifts will make room for me. These gifts are the treasure that God placed inside of me. Because I was trying to fit the mold of what others wanted me to be I second guessed them. I saw myself as a failure because of past mistakes and sins. Not truly understanding that once I have been forgiven. God remembers them no more. As far as the east is to the west, He has removed our transgressions. (Psalm 103:12). But fitting the mold of someone else or just playing with the top layer of dirt, you are reminded of your sins and failures. Because you haven't started to dig deep it will look like you've done anything. Just playing with that top layer of dirt is just rearranging it. Nothing truly changed other than the position it was in. But once you start to dig. That digging gets deeper and deeper. The excitement comes because you start to see changes happening. Digging becomes it's not my will Lord but your will be done my life. Whatever that looks like Lord I'm yours. So, DIG!

What is the best place to start your dig, but learn what you've been covering up. Understand that some things you might uncover may trigger some past experience, past pain and past hurts. I encourage seeking wise counsel. Digging may bring up some things that you thought you would never uncover. I urge you to employ the Holy Spirit before you start to uncover. Because you are going to need Him as your guide, intercessor, strength, counselor, friend, teacher, protector, and guide.

Digging deep is uncovering the real you that you had buried. Are you really ready to dig deep? To get there you'll have to face the past that you may have not forgiven yet. That could be people, places, or things. You've buried something so deep you have to dig and dig and keep digging to find who you are and who you have been created to be, not who you are existing to be.

I remember sitting in this brand experience summit. The question was asked by one of the speakers "What's in your Dirt?"

This question cuts deep because a lot of times what's in our dirt will keep us from digging deep or becoming the person God has designed us to be. In his image and likeness. (Genesis 1:27) Digging deep can paralyze you for a second. May even cause you to shrink back. In that dirt could lay insecurities, fear, identity crisis, lack of self- worth, past hurts, self-sabotage, self-doubt and sins. But you have to Mine that dirt and mining that dirt won't always look or be pleasant. You are going to get dirty and it's going to be messy. The real you is buried in that dirt. Have you ever seen a picture of miners after they have been working in the mines? They are filthy but they did what it takes to get the job done. To find the priceless jewel or that thing of value. You are of value; you are worth mining.

You are Authentically created, sincerely put together in the mind of Christ. Never meant to fit the mold of someone else's identity. Don't commit suicide trying to fit the mold of someone else let's dig deep into your dirt to become the person God designed and created you to be. Are you ready to take this journey of digging deep and becoming the person God designed you to be?

Questions to Ponder:

Do you Believe?

_____

_____

_____

_____

_____

_____

_____

What does your Shrink back look like?

_____

_____

_____

_____

_____

_____

_____

What has Caused you to Shrink Back from digging deep in your dirt?

_____

_____

_____

_____

_____

_____

Do you understand how important you are in the eyes of God?

_____

_____

_____

_____

_____

_____

Do you really know what could be in your dirt?

_____

_____

_____

_____

_____

_____

Prayer

Abba Father, we thank you! Digging in our dirt is about to become real messy so Father; Holy Spirit we need you to be our counselor and guide guy. To be the light upon our feet and you lamp on this path. Give us strength to keep digging until we hit the gold which is the person, he designed us to be. You said you create us in your image and thought of us before the creation of the world. We know everything that you created is good God it's real good. You designed us to be authentic, unique, whole, separate from this world. As we start this dig Father give us the strength to keep going and become the Kingdom citizen. Lord, I thank you as we step into the pleasantries of who he designed us to be. Amen

Reflection

"A fool who does his foolish act again is like a
dog that turns back to what he has thrown up"
Proverbs 6:11 NLV

Beverly Davis was born March13,1970 mother of three and grandmother of one. She is an author, hairstylist, owner of Beautessbybev and a travel agent. Her favorite pass time is journaling and listening to music. She is passionate about serving others and she loves fashion. She recently discovered her purpose is to help women in all walks of life especially middle-aged women as herself, to know that we still have purpose and a life to Live after divorce, after our kids have grown up. God still have purpose for our lives. Our Latter will be Greater than our former.

OVERCOMING FEAR

W hat is Fear? An unpleasant emotion by the belief that something or someone is in dangerous, likely to cause pain or be a threat (*oxford online dictionary*). As a little girl, I would always say I can't wait until I get grown and move out on my own, not knowing all the responsibilities that came along with adulting. I knew I wanted to one day be a wife and have kids and live happily ever after, but I realized later in life that's only on tv. My mother would say, be a child as long as you can, I felt that she was saying that cause she wanted me to stay a little girl forever. Once I completed high school, I realized that adulting was so much more than being a wife, mom, or having a career. It was full of the unknown and life came with trials and tribulations that was design to push you to your God given purpose. That alone made me become fearful and full of anxiety. As far as I can remember I would always worry about anything. I worried about kids not liking me in school because I had long hair, worried about making good grades in school, worried about what people think of me, worried about not being a daddy's girl. I just worried about anything I could image, not realizing that worry and fear was causing life to be all scrambled and wrapped up like a mummy. I became so fearful that my mind became very cloudy. The word of God says so as man thinketh so is he Proverbs 23:7. Because I allowed fear to control my mind, I became restless and always felt like something was wrong or going to happen. I would see my mother do the same thing worry about everything and everybody and I would say Mama that's not your problem, stop worrying, and slowly I was becoming my mom, I even told my mom that I won't allow worrying about other people's problem consume me, but I unknowingly did.

I lost my first brother in a car accident at 21 years old, I was devasted to see my brother being pronounced dead at the scene and put in a black bag, not even today 20 years later I can envision it in my mind. I can honestly say at that moment I knew my life had changed forever. I was mad, hurt and later became bitter because I couldn't understand why my brother was taken away at a very young age. Fear and anxiety because a part of my daily routine, fear that I may die next, fear of losing my other brothers, and fear of life itself not knowing what mine even looked like or not even wanting to live anymore. I remember wanting to end my life because dealing with my brother's death was so hard. I could eat or sleep didn't have a personal relationship with God and I saw my mother in so much pain from the loss of her son. I remember saying God how did this happen; he was a good guy he didn't deserve to die. My other brothers were devasted because it was nothing, they could do to save him. We all were drowning in our sorrow. I remember crying out to God asking him to please take the pain away, after countless nights of crying out to God I heard a still small voice say come to me and give me all your heavy and burdens and I will give you rest (Matthew 11:28). Seek and you will find and knock, and the door will be opened. Not fully understanding the voice of God, I felt a calmness in my spirit, and I begin to rest in the presence of God.

1 Peter 5:7 says Cast your cares on the Lord, because He cares for you. Just give God all of your fears and anxiety and let him carry it. Trust me I know that it's easier said than done, and it definitely don't happen

overnight. Just know that God will give you peace that surpasses all understanding, God really is a keeper, but you have to want to be kept. Living in fear causes your life to become stagnant, paralyzed, and hopeless. That's not how God wants his children to live. He wants us to live life and live it more abundantly. We have to learn to live by faith over fear. My life has been full of ups and downs, but God has never turned his back on me. Every time shows up in your mind, cast it down and replace it with the word of God, God has not given us the spirit of fear but love, power, and a sound mind. Seek God with your whole heart, spend time in his presence and allow him to order your steps, Fear can't reside where the holy spirit lives. So, I challenge each of you to walk by faith and not by sight, knowing that God is with you when you go through the unseen.

Questions to Ponder:

Do you allow fear to control your life?

_____

_____

_____

_____

_____

_____

_____

How much time to spend in God's presence?

_____

_____

_____

_____

_____

_____

Are you casting all of your burdens to God and picking them back up?

_____

_____

_____

_____

_____

_____

Prayer

Heavenly father we come before you asking that you remove the spirit of fear, we cast it down and out in the name of Jesus, it will no longer hold us hostage in the name of Jesus, Thank you Lord for being a lamp unto our feet and a light unto our pathway, as we walk into purpose that you have destined for us in Jesus name Amen.

Reflection

_____

_____

_____

_____

_____

_____

_____

_____

_____

_____

_____

_____

_____

_____

_____

_____

_____

_____

_____

_____

_____

_____

_____

_____

_____

_____

"For God did not give us a spirit of fear. He gave us a spirit of power and of love and of a good mind."
2nd Timothy 1:7 NLV

T.TyRell is a writer and poet who writes inspirational pieces about real-life & black women experiences. First published at the age of ten in *Anthology of Poetry for Young American 1993 Edition*, her love for writing is everlasting. Rooted in Columbia, South Carolina, she is the mother of three sons and a grandmother to a beautiful granddaughter. A small business owner and nonprofit organizer, she has a passion for creating, teaching, and inspiring women and children. Before jumping back into writing, she's worked as a small minority business financial consultant and has completed her BA in Business Administration, AS in Criminal Justice and is current working on her MBA with a minor in Entrepreneurship.

GETTING COMFORTABLE WITH BEING UNCOMFORTABLE

~ele~

Often, we find ourselves in a place of stagnation. A place of routine and repetition. Moving into our purpose is a phrase often used but a task rarely embarked on and more often abandoned. When we began to dig deeper into our "faith walk", purpose and destiny usually take us down a road of uncomfortable changes and decisions. This is called growth. If being able to grow is change, how do we become comfortable with being uncomfortable?

F.A.I.T.H!

Fragility. Acceptance. Indivisible. Triumph. Hope

James 2:17 teaches us "even so faith if it hath not works, is dead." Our faith work is detailed in our drive for change, our ambition for the better, and our walk towards purpose. Demonstrating fragility is our way of giving God all of our broken pieces and knowing He's going to put them back together with precision.

Acceptance is knowing that our faith walk would not be possible without God's grace and mercy. Accepting God's guidance and His will is key on our journey of digging deeper.

Indivisibility is accepting and demonstrating an inseparable longing for God's unchanging, unwavering love. Understanding that nothing and no one should, could, or would stand a chance of separating you from God's hand.

God's grace and mercy provide a victory and triumph above all. When we decide to walk God's path, accept His will and way, we are triumphant.

Hope is the expectation and desire or God's promises to be achieved and come to fruition.

Getting comfortable in being uncomfortable is the belief that God will never leave your side. Getting comfortable in being uncomfortable is walking on God's path without knowing where the road will end. Digging deeper in our faith is the understanding that the mustard seed planted within is going to birth greatness the size of nations. Digging deeper into our faith is understanding that we have to exercise faith and not flesh. When we are faithful to the knowledge that God supplies all of our needs and we are granted the pleasure of purpose. Destiny-driven results and not flesh-fueled moments.

The moment I knew I had to get comfortable with being uncomfortable...

After a long weekend of not being seen, my then-husband came home, intoxicated, and driven to make a point, that I was nothing without him and that he "made me who I was". After being shacked up with his mistress for the long MLK weekend, he decided he'd come home, talk to her while lying in our bed and call me everything but the worthy, loving, supportive wife I was.

It was at the moment that he and I were coming to blows and my two younger sons stood screaming, crying, and pleading for us to stop, that I knew my journey of becoming comfortable with being uncomfortable was about to begin.

With two kids in tow, not knowing where we were going to stay that night, I left with the clothes on my back, tears in my eyes, and veins filled with boiling blood.

Screaming inside, I prayed that if God made a way for me to not have to go back to that alcoholic, narcissistic man, I'd do whatever it was He required of me. One week in a hotel, three weeks living in a friend's spare home, and exactly 30 days later, I closed on the home that I now refer to as my escape route and freedom train. Nearly four years later, the narcissistic alcoholic monster still taunts and haunts me, by my faith allowed me to walk away, unharmed, stronger, and with a testimony bigger than the life he tried to take away. Digging deeper allowed me to grow, live and inspire. Because the faith of a mustard seed showed me, I was more than he called me, I was the daughter of a King, I'm here today to share my testimony, "Life after the D: Defeat into Destiny", coming soon!

Questions to Ponder:

How do you find comfort in the unknown?

_____

_____

_____

_____

_____

_____

_____

What is your "F.A.I.T.H" acronym?

_____

_____

_____

_____

_____

_____

When enough is enough, how does your faith speak to you? Does it encourage you or confuse you?

_____

_____

_____

_____

_____

_____

Prayer

Dear God,

As every reader holds this book, I pray that you provide peace, patience, and understanding. Lord give them the discernment to know when it's you and when it's not. Provide the ability to practice faith and not flesh. Lord, I ask that each reader be guided and shielded with love, grace, and mercy. In your name, Father, amen!

Reflection

_____

_____

_____

_____

_____

_____

_____

_____

_____

_____

_____

_____

_____

_____

_____

_____

_____

_____

_____

_____

_____

_____

_____

_____

"Agree with Him in all your ways, and He
will make your paths straight."
Proverbs 3:6

In 2017 Denysha's marriage abruptly ended and left her a single mother with no plan. This was her moment of rock bottom and also the breaking point for her path to be redirected. Her experience left her knowing shame, fear, self- doubt, low confidence, and abandonment all too well. But she knew her feelings didn't compare to the way of thinking she wanted to embrace. Before Denysha could really change her circumstance, she had to face her hidden places and do the work. She's had to tear down and uproot to break free from mental bondage. Denysha believes in order to become free we must trust our journey and go through the process to be made whole.

THE JOURNEY WITHIN

A t some time or another on this life journey you will be tested. I suppose it's to see how much you have learned through various experiences. Or perhaps it's to actually teach you a lesson, one that causes you to look within and learn something about yourself. I've had many lessons and have taken several tests. But one of the most challenging was learning how to navigate after a failed marriage. My experience of a failed marriage brought to the surface underlying issues I didn't know were there. From abandonment and co-dependency to guilt and shame. The only thing I knew to do initially was to suppress my emotions and dive headfirst into survival mode. Which in turn only stirred up more internal conflict. I eventually had to realize that what I was searching for would not be found in anything outside of myself, I had to dig deep. I had to go within and began to sort out my mess. It was time to stop avoiding the damaged emotions, thoughts, and feelings that I was hoarding. The reality is that I was wanting to add things of value into my life, but I had no space. My heart space was cluttered and bruised with the residue of heartache and pain. There were even some broken pieces that desperately needed mending. It was time to do the work.

How's your heart space? What area(s) in your life needs your attention?

_____

_____

_____

_____

_____

_____

On my journey I have realized that my spirit always had a knowing of what I needed, but because of the distractions that I had allowed into my life I didn't always get the memo. While searching your heart you will need to be honest with yourself. Ask the hard questions! We too often expect the people in our lives to keep it real with us when we don't keep it real with ourselves. I was the person who was struggling internally but I didn't want those around me to know. I convinced myself that the image, what people saw, was more important than ME the actual person! I also thought that no one would understand the mounting mess I was facing, probably because I didn't understand it myself. I discounted my thoughts and feelings and hid them in the dark corners of my heart. Eventually, I couldn't contain the buildup, and it came busting out in the form of anxiety attacks. I had waited too long to clean up my heart space and by this time my heart was screaming for attention. I had to sit with myself and started taking inventory of people, places and things that had contributed to the mess and began to put things in order and serve eviction notices. There was tearing down old ways of thinking, uprooting toxic behaviors and unlearning dysfunctional patterns.

Note to Self

Start to assign the different areas of your life meaning and levels of importance and proceed in that order. If something no longer resonates with you, discontinue use by discarding it.

Questions to Ponder:

What thought processes and behaviors do you need to change?

_____

_____

_____

_____

_____

_____

What beliefs do you need to re-evaluate?

_____

_____

_____

_____

_____

Are you showing up with your mask on? Sis, this is not a costume party! We want the real you.

_____

_____

_____

_____

_____

Are there conversations that need to be had?

_____

_____

_____

_____

_____

_____

(If having an actual conversation is not possible write a letter. You can also talk it out as if they were in the room with you, use the voice notes on your phone. Either way, get it out! My personal favorite, get you a therapist!)

Forgiveness is very important on this journey, but you will have to forgive YOU first. Trust me it's difficult to forgive anyone when you still holding a grudge against yourself. Learn to listen to your intuition, your god voice, your internal compass. Be patient with yourself, give yourself grace and show yourself compassion. Self-love is going to be essential while digging up all those lies you buried about yourself. I had been so entangled in others' perception of me I forgot who I really was and what it felt like to be whole. I only saw the used and damaged version of me. I believed less in my true self and more in the false version. Be who you are not who you think you're supposed to be. Healing takes time. Some of us have some deep wounds that are infected or broken that need resetting. Keep in mind this work of digging up can and probably will get messy but you have been equipped with everything you need to complete this renovation and restore your heart space.

How do you show up for yourself?

_____

_____

_____

_____

_____

_____

What is your internal dialogue like? Is it loving?

_____

_____

_____

_____

_____

_____

Finally, I'll close with this, after you go through the process of digging deep and uprooting the weeds, you have also begun the process of cultivating good planting ground. You now have the space to plant new seeds that will grow and bare good fruit as long as you tend to the garden of your heart by watering and nurturing it, take your time with you. You are beautiful and worth the effort.

Denysha Lavelle

Reflection

_____
_____
_____
_____
_____
_____
_____
_____
_____
_____
_____
_____
_____
_____
_____
_____
_____
_____
_____
_____
_____
_____
_____
_____

Whew! After reading all of the stories from each woman from different walks of life you realize you are not the only one "going through" or has "been through." Life is tough, and no one ever said it would be easy. But when you have a calling and purpose on your life you will face some obstacles. The thing to remember is that it will all be worth it in the end if you continue to push through with the purpose inside of you. Are we saying don't cry? Are we saying you have to exhibit super strength at all times? No, we are not saying that, but what we are saying is take the time, the moment to grieve, to cry, to be silent then get up and keep pushing. What we are saying is you may not be able to do it alone, therefore, reach out to a friend, a pastor, or counselor to help you overcome the internal and external battles against yourself. Remember we are not fighting against flesh but powers and spirts unseen. God wants us to put on the full amour that he has given us to fight against these principalities. The message bible translation puts it best, Ephesians 6:10-12"And that about wraps it up. God is strong, and he wants you strong. So, take everything the Master has set out for you, well-made weapons of the best materials. And put them to use so you will be able to stand up to everything the Devil throws your way. This is no weekend war that we'll walk away from and forget about in a couple of hours. This is for keeps, a life-or-death fight to the finish against the Devil and all his angels.

Thank you for taking the time to read our stories. We hope that by sharing our testimonies it will help you push through your stretching seasons. We know that every story will not end up with the same results, but we do pray that you take note of the steps we made to get to where we are now. May God's grace continue to cover you. Blessing and Peace from us all.

Booking Information

Coletta Bethea
Email: colettaranellcollc@gmail.com
www.colettaranellco.com
IG: @ladycspeaks

D'Jare Campbell
Email: info@djarecampbell.com
www.DjareCampbell.com

Beverly Davis
Email: Mrsdiva.bd@gmail.com
Beauteesbybev@myshopify.com

Tatecca Allen
Email: queensleadnp@gmail.com

Denysha Lavelle
Email: denysha.lavelle@gmail.com
IG: @Denysha.Lavelle

Quantissa Smith
Email: Authenticphase2@gmail.com
www.authentic2.com

REFERENCES

Please notes scriptural references are taken from the New Life Version (NLV), The Passion Translation (TPT), New King James Version (NKJV), God's Word Translation (GW), English Standard Version (ESV), and The Message Bible Translation (MSG). Some scriptures have been paraphrased but does reference the correct biblical passage.